A Paines Plough Production

G000080137

The Initiate

by Alexandra Wood

The first performance of *The Initiate* took place on
2 August 2014 in the Paines Plough Roundabout at
Summerhall, Edinburgh

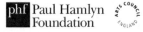

The Initiate

by Alexandra Wood

Cast

Man	Andrew French
Younger Man	Abdul Salis
Woman	Siân Reese-Williams

Creative Team

Direction	George Perrin
Design	Lucy Osborne
Lighting Design	Emma Chapman
Sound Design	Tom Gibbons
Movement Director	Kate Sagovsky
Associate Director	Sean Linnen
Associate Sound Design	Dom Kennedy
Assistant Movement Director	Jennifer Jackson
Dialect Coaches	Helen Ashton
	Richard Ryder
Producer	Hanna Streeter
Touring Production Manager	Rachel Shipp
Production Manager	Bernd Fauler
Company Stage Manager	Harriet Stewart
Assistant Producer	Francesca Moody

Paines Plough would like to thank the following for their support on the production:

Dr Ryan Jablonski from the London School of Economics

ALEXANDRA WOOD (Writer)

Alexandra's plays include an adaptation of Jung Chang's *Wild Swans* (ART/Young Vic); *The Empty Quarter* (Hampstead); *The Centre* (Islington Community Theatre); *Decade* (co-writer, Headlong); *Unbroken* (Gate); *The Lion's Mouth* (Royal Court Rough Cuts); *The Eleventh Capital* (Royal Court) and the radio play *Twelve Years* (BBC Radio 4). She is a winner of the George Devine Award and was the Big Room Playwright-in-residence at Paines Plough in 2013.

ANDREW FRENCH (Man)

Theatre credits include: *The Flesh is Mine* (Border Crossings); *The Jungle Book, Refugee Boy* (West Yorkshire Playhouse); *Julius Caesar* (RSC); *Six Characters in Search of an Author, A Midsummer Night's Dream* (Aquila Theatre USA); *Measure for Measure* (Almeida); *Our Friends in the North* (Northern Stage); *Monster* (Royal Exchange, Manchester); *I Like Mine With a Kiss* (Bush); *As You Like It* (Wyndham's, London); *Reference to Salvador Dali…* (Arcola/Young Vic, London); *Titus Andronicus* (The Project, Dublin); *The Taming of the Shrew* (Nottingham Playhouse); *The Ramayana* (National Theatre/Birmingham Repertory); *Merchant of Venice, Troilus and Cressida* (National Theatre); *The Merchant of Venice* (Shakespeare's Globe); *The Taming of the Shrew* (English Touring Theatre); *Things Fall Apart* (West Yorkshire Playhouse/Royal Court); *The Tempest* (Nottingham Playhouse); *The Tempest* (Shared Experience).

Film credits include: *Artificial Horizon* (Artificial Horizon Limited); *Breaking the Bank* (Black Hangar Studios); *F2014* (Thelma Films/Leuviah Film); *Song for Marion* (WH Films); *Weapon* (MPCA Films); *Exorcist: The Beginning* (Morgan Creek); *Exorcist: Dominion* (Morgan Creek USA); *Beyond Borders* (Mandalay Pictures); *The Merchant of Venice* (BBC Films); *Doctor Sleep* (Kismet Films); *Tailor of Panama* (Columbia Pictures); *Let's Stick Together* (Indio Pictures Limited).

TV credits include: *EastEnders, Holby City, Doctors, Casualty* (BBC); *Perfect Parents* (Granada/ITV); *Primeval* (Impossible Pictures/ITV); *Soundproof, Blast!* (Films/BBC2); *The Bill, Burnside* (Thames Television); *Trust* (Box TV); *In Deep* (Valentine Productions); *A Touch of Frost* (Yorkshire Television); *Family Affairs* (Pearson Television); *Tough Love* (Granada).

Radio credits include: *The Mother Of…* (BBC Radio 4); *The Last Supper* (BBC Radio 3).

ABDUL SALIS (Younger Man)

Theatre credits include: *Joe Guy* (Tiata Fahodzi); *Exonnerated, War Horse* (National Theatre); *Don Juan in Soho* (Donmar Warehouse); *Henry V* (Unicorn).

TV credits include: *Doctors* (Blunt Pictures); *Hacks, Outnumbered, Trevor's World of Sport* (Hat Trick Productions); *Strike Back* (Left Bank Pictures); *Victoria Wood Christmas Special* (Phil McIntyre Productions); *Casualty* (BBC); *M.I. High* (Kudos For BBC); *The Bill* (Talkback Thames); *Doctor Who* (BBC/DW Productions); *Gifted* (Red Productions); *Roger Roger* (BBC); *The Hidden City* (Hallmark Entertainment).

Film credits include: *Fly Boys* (Electric Entertainments); *Animal* (Animal Productions); *Sahara* (Sahara Productions); *Welcome Home* (Wega-Film); *Love, Actually* (DNA/Working Title).

Radio includes: *Skyvers* (BBC Radio 3)

SIÂN REESE-WILLIAMS (Woman)

Theatre credits include: *Enjoy* (West Yorkshire Playhouse); *Children of Fate* (Bussey Building); *Be My Baby* (New Vic Theatre); *As You Like It* (Derby Playhouse); the *Future Perfect* season (Paines Plough/Rose Bruford); *Coltan* (Paines Plough); *Sixty Five Miles* (Paines Plough/Hull Truck); *Diamond* (King's Head); *The Dreaming* (National Youth Music Theatre); *Into the Woods* (National Youth Music Theatre).

TV credits include: *Emmerdale* (ITV); *Cowbois Ac Injians* (Opus TF).

GEORGE PERRIN (Direction)

George Perrin is the joint Artistic Director of Paines Plough. He was formerly co-founder and Joint Artistic Director of Nabokov and Trainee Associate Director at Paines Plough and Watford Palace Theatre.

Directing credits for Paines Plough include *Seawall* by Simon Stephens (National Theatre Shed); *Good With People* by David Harrower (59East59 Theatres New York/Traverse/Orán Mòr); *London* by Simon Stephens (national tour); *Sixty Five Miles* by Matt Hartley (Hull Truck); *The 8th* by Che Walker and Paul Heaton (Latitude Festival/Barbican/ Manchester International Festival/national tour); *Dig* by Katie Douglas and *Juicy Fruits* by Leo Butler (Orán Mòr/national tour) .

As Trainee Associate Director of Paines Plough, directing credits include *House of Agnes* by Levi David Addai; *The Dirt Under the Carpet* by Rona Munro; *Crazy Love* by Che Walker; *My Little Heart Dropped in Coffee* by Duncan Macmillan and *Babies* by Katie Douglas.

Further directing credits include *2nd May 1997* by Jack Thorne (Bush); *Terre Haute* by Edmund White (59East59 Theatres New York/West End/national tour/ Assembly Rooms, Edinburgh Festival Fringe); *Is Everyone Ok?* and *Public Displays of Affection* by Joel Horwood and *Camarilla* by Van Badham (Nabokov).

LUCY OSBORNE (Design)

Lucy's previous designs for Paines Plough include *An Intervention*, *Jumpers For Goalposts* (also Hull Truck/Watford Palace Theatre and Bush Theatre); The Roundabout Seasons (2011 and 2012) and *Love Love Love* (also Royal Court/national tour).

Her many other theatre designs include *Privacy*, *Coriolanus*, *Berenice* and *The Recruiting Officer* (Donmar Warehouse); *In the Vale of Health*, *Hello/Goodbye* and *Blue Heart Afternoon* (Hampstead Theatres); *Translations*, *Plenty*, *The Unthinkable*, *The Long and the Short and the Tall* (Sheffield Theatres); *The Machine* (Manchester International Festival/NYC); *Huis Clos* (Donmar Trafalgar season); *Twelfth Night* (Winner of the Chicago 'Jeff Award' for Scenic Design); *The Taming of the Shrew* (Chicago Shakespeare Theatre); *Peter Pan* (Sherman Cymru); *Precious Little Talent* (Trafalgar Studios) and *Shades* (Royal Court).

As an Associate Artist at the Bush Theatre her work included *The Aliens*, *Like a Fishbone*, *The Whisky Taster*, *If There Is I Havent Found It Yet*, *Wrecks*, *Tinderbox*, *Sea Wall* and the *Broken Space* season.

EMMA CHAPMAN (Lighting Design)

Emma Chapman trained at Bristol Old Vic Theatre School.

Theatre credits in recent seasons include: *Donkeys' Years* (Rose Theatre, Kingston); Schools' Theatre Festival 2014, *Parallel Hamlet* (Young Vic); *Run* (Polka); *Dublin Carol* (Donmar season); *Sex With a Stranger* with Russell Tovey and Jaime Winston (Trafalgar Studios); the acclaimed production of O'Neill's *Three Sea Plays* in the Old Vic Tunnels; *Dick Whittington* in Bury St Edmunds; three plays for Paines Plough's Roundabout in Sheffield (seen in London later that year); and *Rose* with Art Malik at Edinburgh.

Opera credits include: *Il Turco in Italia* (Angers/Nantes Opera); *Xerxes* and *Carmen* (Royal Northern College of Music, Manchester); *Così fan tutte* (Royal College of Music); *The Pied Piper* (Opera North).

She has also lit *Rumplestiltskin* for London Children's Ballet at the Peacock Theatre, available on DVD.

Other notable engagements include the Olivier Award-winning play *The Mountaintop* for Theatre503 and at the Trafalgar Studio; the highly praised *The Painter* which opened the new Arcola Theatre, and the David Mamet double bill at the Arcola Studio; *Wet Weather Cover* at the King's Head and Arts Theatre; *The Machine Gunners* and *The Planet and Stuff* at Polka Theatre; two plays and two comedy shows for Invisible Dot at the 2013 Edinburgh Festival.

Future work includes the new Roundabout theatre making its debut in Edinburgh.

TOM GIBBONS (Sound Design)

Tom trained at Central School of Speech and Drama.

Recent theatre includes *The White Devil*, *As You Like It* (RSC); *Translations* (Sheffield Crucible); *A View From the Bridge*, *Happy Days*, *A Season in the Congo*, *Disco Pigs* (Young Vic); *Mr Burns*, *1984* (Almeida); *Romeo and Juliet* (Headlong); *Lion Boy* (Complicite); *Julius Caesar* (Donmar Warehouse/St Ann's, Brooklyn); *Grounded* (Gate); *The Spire*

(Salisbury Playhouse); *London* (Paines Plough); *Roundabout* season (Shoreditch Town Hall, Paines Plough); *The Rover* (Hampton Court Palace); *Love Love Love* (Royal Court); *Island* (National Theatre/tour); *Dead Heavy Fantastic* (Liverpool Everyman); *Plenty* (Crucible Studio, Sheffield); *Encourage the Others* (Almeida); *Wasted* (Paines Plough/tour); *Chalet Lines, The Knowledge, Little Platoons, 50 Ways to Leave Your Lover* (Bush); *Hairy Ape, Shivered, Faith, Hope And Charity, The Hostage, Toad* (Southwark Playhouse); *Sold* (Theatre503); *The Chairs* (Ustinov, Bath); *The Country, The Road to Mecca, The Roman Bath, 1936, The Shawl* (Arcola); *Utopia, Bagpuss, Everything Must Go, Soho Streets* (Soho); *Hitchcock Blonde* (Hull Truck).

As Associate: *Choir Boy* (Royal Court); *Broken Space Season* (Bush).

KATE SAGOVSKY (Movement Director)
Kate trained in Dance Studies at Laban after completing an MA in Movement Studies at the Royal Central School of Speech and Drama, and a degree in English Literature at Oxford University. She works across theatre, dance and live art as a director and movement director/choreographer.

Kate has worked widely as a movement director, including on productions at Theatre Royal Stratford East, BAC, the Bush, Oxford Playhouse, Tristan Bates and Theatre503. She worked as the Resident Movement Practitioner at the Royal Shakespeare Company for the 2011 season, including movement direction on *The Homecoming* (dir. David Farr) and *Mojo* (dir. Justin Audibert). She continues to work for the RSC as a Freelance Movement Practitioner and Education Associate Practitioner. She has also taught as a lecturer in Actor-Movement at many UK Drama Schools, at AFDA Film School (Cape Town, South Africa) and for Shakespeare's Globe.

As Artistic Director of MOVING DUST Kate creates cross-art-form performance that has toured to theatre and dance festivals around the UK [www.movingdust.com]. Other productions as director include *A Midsummer Night's Dream* (Cambridge Arts Theatre); *Love's Labour's Lost* (Metropolitan Arts Centre, Tokyo/UK tour).

Work as Associate Director (Movement) includes: *Eska's English Skies* (Queen Elizabeth Hall, Southbank Centre) and *GVE* with Matthew Herbert Big Band (Barbican/Glastonbury). She has also worked as a Staff Director at the National Theatre.

SEAN LINNEN (Associate Director)
Sean is currently undertaking a Trainee Artistic Directorship in partnership with Sheffield Theatres and Paines Plough after receiving funding from Arts Council England in December 2013.

Prior to this he was a Staff Director at the National Theatre and Assistant Director to Josie Rourke on *The Machine* by Matt Charman for the Donmar Warehouse, Manchester International Festival and Park Avenue Armory, New York.

Directing credits include *A Preoccupation With Romance* by Beth Grant (Edinburgh Festival Fringe); *Hollow* by Beth Grant (Bike Shed Theatre, Exeter); *Hi-Vis* by Clara Brennan and *Fragile* by David Greig (Theatre Uncut/Sheffield Theatres).

Other assistant director credits include *Translations* by Brian Friel (ETT/Rose Theatre, Kingston/Sheffield Theatres); *The Daughter-In-Law* by D.H. Lawrence; *A Taste of Honey* by Shelagh Delaney and *Copenhagen* by Michael Frayn (Sheffield Theatres).

DOM KENNEDY (Associate Sound Design)
Dominic Kennedy is a sound designer and composer for performance and live events; he has a keen interest in developing new work and implementing sound design from an early stage of a process. Dominic is a graduate from RCSSD where he developed specialist skills in collaborative and devised theatre-making. Dominic has recently designed shows and collaborated with Jamie Wood, Gameshow, Engineer, Choon Ping, Outbox, Jemima James and Mars Tarrab. Recent associate design roles include *War Correspondents* by Song Theatre.

JENNIFER JACKSON (Assistant Movement Director)

Jennifer trained at East 15 and works as an actor, deviser and movement director.

Theatre credits include: *Thérèse Raquin* (Bath Theatre Royal); *Scenes From an Execution* (National Theatre); *Death and the Maiden* (West End); *Humbug, Flathampton* (Royal & Derngate Theatre; winner of Argus Angel for Artistic Excellence at Brighton Festival 2013); *Sonnet Walks* (Shakespeare's Globe); *Remote Control* (National Theatre Studio); *Soon Until Forever, Red Shoes* (Theatre503); *Amphibians, The Drawing Play* (Offstage Theatre); *Fixer* (Ovalhouse); *Moshing* (Arcola); *The Box* (Bush/Moving Dust). Jennifer is an associate artist with Tangled Feet. Productions include: *All That is Solid Melts into Air* (National Theatre); *Push, Inflation* (Lyric Hammersmith); *Remote Control* (National Theatre Studio), and *Care* (National Theatre Studio/ARC Stockton).

Movement direction includes: *Debris* (Southwark Playhouse/Openworks Theatre); *Macbeth in Original Pronunciation* (Passion in Practice/Sam Wanamaker Playhouse); *Gut Girls* (Brockley Jack); *Corpus Christi* (The Space); *Be My Baby* (GAP Salon/Etcetera Theatre).

Paines Plough

'Revered touring company Paines Plough' *Time Out*

Paines Plough is the UK's national theatre of new plays. We commission and produce the best playwrights and tour their plays far and wide. Whether you're in Liverpool or Lyme Regis, Scarborough or Southampton, a Paines Plough show is coming to a theatre near you soon.

'The lifeblood of the UK's theatre ecosystem' *Guardian*

Paines Plough was formed in 1974 over a pint of Paines bitter in the Plough pub. Since then we've produced more than 130 new productions by world-renowned playwrights like Stephen Jeffreys, Abi Morgan, Sarah Kane, Mark Ravenhill, Dennis Kelly and Mike Bartlett. We've toured those plays to hundreds of places from Manchester to Moscow to Maidenhead.

'That noble company Paines Plough, de facto national theatre of new writing' *Telegraph*

We celebrate 40 years of Paines Plough in 2014 with our our biggest, boldest, furthest-reaching programme of work ever. Programme 2014 sees 10 productions touring to 50 places around the UK, featuring the work of 100 playwrights.

'I think some theatre just saved my life' @kate_clement on Twitter

Paines Plough Limited is a company limited by guarantee and a registered charity.
Registered Company no: 1165130
Registered Charity no: 267523

Paines Plough, 4th Floor, 43 Aldwych, London WC2B 4DN
+ 44 (0) 20 7240 4533
office@painesplough.com
www.painesplough.com

 Follow @PainesPlough on Twitter

 Like Paines Plough at facebook.com/PainesPloughHQ

Donate to Paines Plough at justgiving.com/PainesPlough

Paines Plough are

Joint Artistic Directors	James Grieve
	George Perrin
Producer	Hanna Streeter
General Manager	Aysha Powell
Assistant Producer	Francesca Moody
Admin and Finance Assistant	Natalie Adams
Marketing Assistant	Benedict Lombe
Trainee Artistic Director	Sean Linnen
Associate Director	Stef O'Driscoll
Production Placement (Birbeck)	Miyuki Kasahara
Interim Administration Assistant	Kate Rayner
Literary Placement	Frances Turpin
Production Manager	Bernd Fauler
Press Representative	Kate Morley

Board of Directors

Caro Newling (Chair), Ola Animashawun, Christopher Bath, Micaela Boas, Tamara Cizeika, Nia Janis, Zarine Kharas, Christopher Millard, Cindy Polemis, Simon Stephens.

Supported by
ARTS COUNCIL ENGLAND

THE INITIATE

Alexandra Wood

Thanks

I'd like to thank Sebastian Born, Purni Morell and the rest of the NT Studio team for giving me the time and space to write this play; Jon Pashley, Andrew French, Ashley Zhangazha and Aïcha Kossoko who allowed me to hear it for the first time; George and James at Paines Plough for giving it a home; Lisa, my agent; the Roundabout actors and production team for their enthusiasm and commitment to the piece.

A.W.

For Kat Wilkins

4

Characters

MAN
YOUNGER MAN
WOMAN

Note on Text

A forward slash in the text (/) indicates a point of interruption.

A lack of a full stop at the end of a line indicates that the speaker cannot or does not want to finish.

This text went to press before the end of rehearsals and so may differ slightly from the play as performed.

Scene One

YOUNGER MAN. How long have you been doing this?

MAN. Long enough.

YOUNGER MAN. Maybe you've been doing it too long, is that the problem?

MAN. It's the quickest route.

YOUNGER MAN. It just isn't.

MAN. Have you tried it?

YOUNGER MAN. I don't need to.

MAN. Maybe you should try it first. It doesn't take as long as you might think.

YOUNGER MAN. I don't have to debate this with you. Sat nav tells me how long things take, and sat nav tells me you're wrong.

MAN. In terms of distance

YOUNGER MAN. It takes longer, that's the point.

MAN. As the crow flies

YOUNGER MAN. Is the crow carrying the passengers from A to B?

MAN. Crows have the highest IQs of all birds.

YOUNGER MAN. So do you think a crow would take the scenic route?

MAN. He does take the scenic route, he flies above it all.

YOUNGER MAN. But given that we can't fly

MAN. We fly all over the world all the time.

YOUNGER MAN. In your car, in your car you can't fly, so
    what would your friend the crow do in that situation? I'll tell
    you what he'd do, he'd do the best he could. Which is not to
    drive through the centre of the city, with all the lights and the
    traffic and the cameras.

MAN. It depends.

YOUNGER MAN. No, it doesn't depend. He'd do the smart
    thing. He'd use the ring roads and the motorways and he'd
    get back to his nest quicker.

MAN. The crow is an innovator. He'd experiment.

YOUNGER MAN. Forget the crow.

MAN. You ask a customer. You ask them if they enjoy the trip,
    they'll tell you.

YOUNGER MAN. That's the problem.

MAN. What problem?

YOUNGER MAN. What the customer wants is to get to his
    destination.

MAN. They get off the plane, they want to see the sights.

YOUNGER MAN. That's not your job.

MAN. Does that mean I can't show them a few sights?

YOUNGER MAN. Yes, that's exactly what it means, now we're
    getting somewhere.

MAN. Every motorway is the same. Every ring road the same.
    Every city has them.

YOUNGER MAN. And why does every city have them?

MAN. Because everyone wants to get everywhere yesterday.

YOUNGER MAN. Because ring roads get you there faster.

MAN. Why drive round and round when you can drive along
    the Thames? When you can drive past the Houses of
    Parliament? Number 10. Buckingham Palace.

YOUNGER MAN. Go sightseeing on your own time.

MAN. People don't come here to sit on the North Circular.

YOUNGER MAN. People come here for all sorts of reasons.

MAN. Who wants to sit on the North Circular?

YOUNGER MAN. No one, but it happens to be part of your job so

MAN. It's my job to drive people from where they are, to where they want to be. I do my job.

YOUNGER MAN. We've lost clients.

MAN. Times are tough.

YOUNGER MAN. Because of you.

MAN. Me?

YOUNGER MAN. Clients ask for other drivers.

MAN. Who?

Pause.

YOUNGER MAN. Look, you're a nice guy. But people don't want a tour of the city, especially when they live in it.

MAN. You can never know a city like this completely. There's always something new to discover.

YOUNGER MAN. When they get in from a stressful business trip they just want to get home or back to the office, they don't want some bloke chatting at them, telling them every fact about everything they pass.

MAN. People enjoy it.

YOUNGER MAN. And they don't want to hear about crows.

MAN. I think Sir David Attenborough would disagree.

YOUNGER MAN. Sir David Attenborough isn't a minicab driver.

Pause.

I can't afford to have drivers I can't send on certain jobs.

MAN. Who are these people? Let me talk to them.

YOUNGER MAN. They've heard enough. Too much, that's the problem.

MAN. Okay, so I'll shut up.

YOUNGER MAN. And drive the fastest route?

MAN. If we're not going to talk, then we have to have something to look at.

I've been here ten years. This was never a problem before.

YOUNGER MAN. Because you used to do what you were told.

MAN. How do you know?

YOUNGER MAN. When I started here, they said yeah he's a good guy. He's professional. You don't have to worry about him.

MAN. You don't.

In ten years, I've only had one accident, and that wasn't my fault. Look at the records.

YOUNGER MAN. It's not your driving I'm worried about.

MAN. Who complained?

YOUNGER MAN. That doesn't matter.

MAN. I'm never late for a client.

YOUNGER MAN. And how do you make sure of that?

MAN. I leave on time.

YOUNGER MAN. And? Do you take the meandering route along the river to the airport?

MAN. No, I take the North Circular.

YOUNGER MAN. So you admit it's quicker?

MAN. Of course it's quicker.

YOUNGER MAN. So why are we even having this conversation?

MAN. This is a beautiful city. This is my city. My beautiful city.

YOUNGER MAN. So join the tourist board, join the Big Bus Company, but you can't do this job any more.

Pause.

If you refuse to take the fast routes and cut out all the chat, I can't afford to keep you on.

MAN. You know I have a family.

YOUNGER MAN. Look maybe when things pick up again I'll give you a call, but for now, I just can't afford to

MAN. Bob's only been in the job a couple of months.

He doesn't have a family.

YOUNGER MAN. He has a wife.

MAN. He doesn't have children.

YOUNGER MAN. Bob drives on whatever road gets him there quickest. No one's complained about Bob.

MAN. That's all they have to complain about? Their driver tries to give them too much information about the city they're in. About where they are.

YOUNGER MAN. Some people don't mind that kind of thing, but others just want to be quiet and if you keep talking at them they feel trapped.

MAN. Trapped?

YOUNGER MAN. I can give you a good reference.

MAN. People feel trapped in my car?

YOUNGER MAN. One woman felt slightly uneasy, shall we say.

MAN. Why?

YOUNGER MAN. She got a fright when you went a route she didn't expect.

MAN. Does she get a fright when her bus is rediverted?

YOUNGER MAN. When she asked you why you were going that way, you told her not to worry, that she'd enjoy the ride.

MAN. And did she?

YOUNGER MAN. When you told her that and then refused to go the way she asked, how do you think she felt?

MAN. Reassured. That I knew the way.

YOUNGER MAN. She got a fright.

MAN. Why?

YOUNGER MAN. She thought you might

MAN. What?

YOUNGER MAN. That you were gonna

MAN. Hurt her?

YOUNGER MAN. She doesn't know you.

Pause.

MAN. Maybe you should give your reference to the police.

YOUNGER MAN. When you take people on your magical mystery tours, you don't help yourself.

MAN. I remember this woman, she didn't say a word, nothing.

YOUNGER MAN. She was frightened.

MAN. Why? I was driving down Grosvenor Road and Millbank, not back alleys.

It was the middle of the day.

Pause.

YOUNGER MAN. If it was just her, then we wouldn't be having this conversation.

MAN. Lots of people think I'm going to kill them?

YOUNGER MAN. Of course not, but there have been complaints.

MAN. Because I talk? In some places that's considered friendly. In some places people enjoy speaking to people and learning new things.

YOUNGER MAN. Perhaps you should drive a cab to one of those places then.

Scene Two

WOMAN. They said there was an accident at Henlys Corner, were you caught up in that?

MAN. No.

WOMAN. I didn't know what time to expect you home.

MAN. I went for a drink.

WOMAN. A drink?

MAN. With a few guys at work.

WOMAN. Why?

MAN. They asked me.

WOMAN. That's nice.

MAN. They didn't know I don't drink. But I thought, first time I've been asked, I'll go.

WOMAN. Was it a special occasion?

MAN. I don't think so.

WOMAN. Did you enjoy it?

MAN. How did Zahi's exam go?

WOMAN. Well.

MAN. He's revising?

WOMAN. Been working all night.

MAN. And Cabaas?

Pause.

WOMAN. He didn't go to school today.

MAN. Is he sick?

WOMAN. He says he's sick.

MAN. Has he got a temperature?

WOMAN. A slight one perhaps.

MAN. Have you taken him to the doctor?

WOMAN. I don't think he's that sick.

MAN. Then he can go to school.

Pause.

Am I wrong?

WOMAN. No.

MAN. But you just let him take the day off?

WOMAN. I get the feeling there's

MAN. What?

WOMAN. He's not lazy. He likes going to school and it would've been boring for him here all day.

MAN. So perhaps he learnt a lesson.

WOMAN. Perhaps he's having trouble.

MAN. He doesn't get involved in that kind of thing.

WOMAN. You don't get the choice with that kind of thing.

MAN. He's a popular boy. And he's got an older brother to protect him.

WOMAN. Zahi's got enough to worry about.

MAN. Cabaas!

WOMAN. Tread carefully.

MAN. Cabaas!

WOMAN. He asked me if he could stay at home, he didn't just skip school like other boys.

MAN. Cabaas!

WOMAN. He might be asleep, he's not been well.

MAN. He's done nothing all day.

YOUNGER MAN *appears*.

How are you?

YOUNGER MAN. Alright.

MAN. Then why weren't you at school?

YOUNGER MAN. I feel better now, but earlier I felt sick.

MAN. Where?

YOUNGER MAN. In my stomach.

MAN. Were you sick?

WOMAN. You'll be able to go to school tomorrow.

MAN. Will you?

Pause.

Zahi's there. You have any problems you go to him. Or a teacher.

YOUNGER MAN. I'm not having problems. I just didn't feel well.

MAN. I thought you liked school.

YOUNGER MAN. I do.

MAN. What did you miss today?

YOUNGER MAN. Biology. Maths. English. Art.

MAN. A businessman needs to know about those things. A doctor needs to know about those things. A lawyer needs to know about those things Cabaas.

YOUNGER MAN. I read ahead in my maths book and did the exercises.

MAN. I thought you were sick.

YOUNGER MAN. When I felt better.

MAN. So maybe all you need to do is stay at home and read all the books and you'll be fine. Would that be better?

You'd never have to speak to anyone.

Pause.

Already you've forgotten how to talk.

YOUNGER MAN. I haven't forgotten how to talk.

MAN. When you start working you won't know what to say to people. You'll be able to do your job, you'll be able to tell them facts and figures and anything they might like to know but will they invite you for a drink after work?

WOMAN. Of course they'll invite him, Cabaas has lots of friends.

MAN. So why's he sick?

WOMAN. He's better now. Aren't you?

Pause.

MAN. You can learn all you like but you won't get a job unless you can speak to people. You come to this country as a doctor and you end up cleaning toilets. Why? Because they don't trust you. Or your so-called qualifications.

YOUNGER MAN. Maybe they shouldn't.

WOMAN. Why shouldn't they trust you?

YOUNGER MAN. People go on holiday and get kidnapped by our people.

Maybe they think we'll do that.

MAN. That's nothing to do with us.

YOUNGER MAN. They think it is.

MAN. Pirates have nothing to do with us.

YOUNGER MAN. They come from where we come from.

MAN. We aren't all pirates.

YOUNGER MAN. They look like us.

MAN. The same colour skin, that's all.

YOUNGER MAN. They might even be related to us.

WOMAN. Of course they aren't.

They're nothing to do with you.

YOUNGER MAN. Have you seen the picture? The one they've been showing everywhere.

WOMAN. Yes, I've seen it.

YOUNGER MAN. With the pirates in the background, pointing AK47s at their heads.

WOMAN. They're just boys most of them. Desperate boys.

YOUNGER MAN. One of them, the one to the right of the old man, he looks just like me.

They've started calling me Blackbeard.

He could be my twin.

WOMAN. We'll talk to the head.

YOUNGER MAN. His eyes

He's pointing the AK47 at the man's head but it looks like he could kill him just with his eyes.

One guy at school gave me a pair of sunglasses and told me he didn't trust my eyes.

WOMAN. It's bullying, we'll report it.

YOUNGER MAN. He looked scared. It's not bullying when he looks more scared than I do.

WOMAN. He knows what he's doing. So you happen to bear a resemblance to a man in this picture

YOUNGER MAN. It's more than a resemblance, he could be my brother.

WOMAN. He's not your brother. You might look similar, but you're nothing like him. You're luckier than him, you've had more opportunities, and can you see now why you have to use them, why you can't be sick again tomorrow Cabaas.

YOUNGER MAN. Can't you do something Dad?

WOMAN. Of course he can, he'll talk to the head.

YOUNGER MAN. To save the couple. The British couple.

Pause.

MAN. I don't know the pirates.

YOUNGER MAN. You're from the same place as them.

You can speak to them.

WOMAN. These men mean business Cabaas, it isn't a game, they'll kill whoever they need to kill.

YOUNGER MAN. They might not. If you speak to them.

Look at me. Am I ruthless? Am I a killer?

Then neither are they.

WOMAN. You haven't kidnapped anyone.

MAN. He doesn't need to.

WOMAN. There are millions of people in Somalia who don't turn to piracy.

MAN. They're probably hungry.

WOMAN. You aren't the same as them Cabaas.

YOUNGER MAN. How can anyone tell?

WOMAN. Just by speaking to you.

YOUNGER MAN. If they bother.

WOMAN. You have more in common with the couple they kidnapped than with the pirates.

YOUNGER MAN. Even Mrs Patricks said it to me. And she's one of the nice ones. Isn't it terrible, she said, the pirates. As if it was a test. Then someone asked if I knew them.

MAN. You've never even lived there.

YOUNGER MAN. I said yeah, it's terrible. It's terrible that the British Government are doing nothing. And she said government is singular Cabaas. The British Government *is* doing nothing. Not *are*.

Scene Three

WOMAN. We don't do that.

MAN. You're a Somali charity.

WOMAN. We don't have enough funds as it is.

MAN. What charity ever has enough funds? You can't let that stop you.

WOMAN. We've had to cancel our weekly group for elderly women.

MAN. They don't have groups for the elderly in Somalia. Because nobody gets to be elderly.

WOMAN. Please don't lecture me.

Anyway you're not asking me to help Somalis.

MAN. That's exactly what I'm asking.

WOMAN. No, you're asking me to give money we don't have to help a British couple.

MAN. You're British too now aren't you?

Pause.

WOMAN. We're small. We run after-school clubs, educational programmes, we don't get involved in things like this.

They say charity begins at home, well this is my home now.

MAN. So you're happy to turn a blind eye?

WOMAN. If the Government isn't helping then why should we?

MAN. Did you sit back and say that when you saw that young Somalis needed after-school clubs and holiday outings? Did you say, oh well the Government doesn't provide it so why should we?

Pause.

WOMAN. We put our limited money into things that make a real difference. Handing it over to pirates on the other side of the world isn't going to make a difference to our lives.

MAN. It could.

WOMAN. Will it help a Somali woman learn English so she can get a job?

MAN. If this couple is killed, who's going to hire a Somali woman anyway?

Pause.

WOMAN. The pirates have nothing to do with us.

MAN. They're Somali, you're Somali.

You want to teach these kids pride in their culture, but that's money down the drain if they then go to school and the only thing their classmates know of Somalia is that they have pirates there.

WOMAN. You give these people money they'll do it again.

MAN. Maybe. But if we can show, even just once, that we stand with this couple, that we'll rally as a community, alongside

them, that we'll do everything we can to save them, don't
you think that'll show them what our culture's about? Don't
you think that'll give our children some pride?

Pause.

WOMAN. They want millions.

MAN. We'll offer what we can.

WOMAN. And if we give them this money and they kill them
anyway?

MAN. Then we tried.

WOMAN. That's not good enough. What we have isn't much
but it can make a difference. A difference perhaps you can't
imagine.

Pause.

MAN. I'm just trying to save these people's lives.

WOMAN. You shrug off millions, as if it's nothing.

MAN. I'm not shrugging it off. It's a lot of money, of course it
is, but if we all contribute, it's not impossible.

WOMAN. And then you shrug it off and say, at least we tried.
Millions of pounds, as if it's nothing to lose.

MAN. It wouldn't be a complete loss.

WOMAN. They'd be dead.

MAN. Yes but

We still would've shown that we can stand together.

WOMAN. Are you trying to make a gesture or save their lives?

Pause.

I'm not giving away one pound of our money to make a
gesture. Maybe you can afford to make gestures but

MAN. Do you think cab drivers are rich?

WOMAN. You and your wife both have jobs. Your sons don't
need our after-school clubs.

MAN. I'm not asking for this money for myself.

WOMAN. You come here asking for help

MAN. Not for me personally.

WOMAN. But you've never once come here and offered help. You could've volunteered, wouldn't that be more meaningful than some PR campaign?

MAN. I just want to try to save their lives.

WOMAN. Why?

MAN. Why do I want to save their lives?

WOMAN. Yes, why?

MAN. Is that a serious question?

WOMAN. Why them?

MAN. I'd do the same for anybody.

WOMAN. No you wouldn't. You don't.

Pause.

MAN. We've had a lot of generous contributions.

WOMAN. Good, then you don't need ours.

There was a whole boat of Chinese hostages last year, you didn't try and save them. Why this couple?

Pause.

MAN. Okay, so I haven't done it before, is that a reason not to start?

Why do you take such exception to this couple?

WOMAN. I've got nothing against them but

There are people here I know I can help.

You think people here care about what the pirates do? It might be in the papers for a couple of days, but they'll forget. The stuff about Somali boys in street gangs they don't forget.

What are you going to do? Leave your job and your family,
fly out there and risk your life to save these people?

Pause.

Isn't there enough to do here?

Scene Four

MAN. Do you remember me?

YOUNGER MAN. You're my uncle.

MAN. You haven't seen me in years.

YOUNGER MAN. You send money.

MAN. I do.

YOUNGER MAN. Of course I remember you.

MAN. Because I'm your uncle, or because I send money?

    Pause.

    I'm sorry if I'm staring, you look so like my father.

    Pause.

    Do you think I'm crazy?

YOUNGER MAN. Why?

MAN. To come here.

    Not to come here, but to come here for, to come here to
speak to the pirates.

YOUNGER MAN. You don't come here for a holiday.

MAN. I'm happy to see you too.

YOUNGER MAN. You send money you don't have to feel
guilty.

MAN. I don't feel guilty.

YOUNGER MAN. You think you can help.

MAN. I hope I can

Not help but

It was an impulsive decision, probably.

YOUNGER MAN. If you thought about it you wouldn't have come.

MAN. Maybe not.

I must say I'm grateful to see a familiar face.

YOUNGER MAN. I can't help you.

MAN. You already have.

YOUNGER MAN. I can't help you more than that.

MAN. I'm sure you can help more than you realise.

Pause.

YOUNGER MAN. Perhaps you think I'm a pirate.

MAN. You're not a pirate.

YOUNGER MAN. Maybe your money helped me buy a speedboat, an AK47 and a bazooka.

MAN. You inherited my father's sense of humour as well.

YOUNGER MAN. These flip-flops, this sarong, they don't come cheap.

Not like those rags you're wearing.

Is that a bulletproof vest under your shirt?

Pause.

Don't you trust me?

MAN. You're family.

Of course I trust you.

YOUNGER MAN. So why are you wearing it?

MAN. I've put on a bit of weight. Too much driving a car around.

YOUNGER MAN. Why are you lying to me if you trust me?

Pause.

MAN. It's a dangerous place.

YOUNGER MAN. It's more dangerous when you lie.

MAN. I promised my wife I'd wear it at all times.

She didn't want me to come back here.

She even threatened to divorce me. But, I said, I might get killed. Why bother with the paperwork? Wait and see if I come back alive then we can talk about divorce.

Pause.

I'll take it off.

YOUNGER MAN. Not on my account.

MAN. It's hot.

YOUNGER MAN. You should keep it on.

Pause.

Who's driving your cab while you're here?

MAN. I drive for a company, they can get by without me.

YOUNGER MAN. What car do you drive?

MAN. A Ford Mondeo. Usually. But sometimes the E-Class Mercedes.

YOUNGER MAN. A Mercedes?

MAN. They're company cars.

YOUNGER MAN. But you have your own car too.

MAN. Yes.

Pause.

YOUNGER MAN. What do you think I spend your money on, if not piracy?

MAN. I wouldn't dictate to you what to spend it on. When I give it to you, it's yours.

YOUNGER MAN. But do you ever think, this is like throwing money away?

Pause.

MAN. I was very sad to hear about your father.

Even though I couldn't be here we observed our own mourning period.

YOUNGER MAN. You could have been here.

You're here now.

MAN. It was a difficult time.

YOUNGER MAN. You're here now to speak to some pirates, but you couldn't come for your brother.

MAN. It was even more dangerous then than it is now.

YOUNGER MAN. You've come here wearing a bulletproof vest. To speak to some pirates.

You look like a journalist.

MAN. I'd like to make some good news.

YOUNGER MAN. Good news for who?

MAN. Everyone. They'll get their money.

YOUNGER MAN. You have the money?

MAN. It's not mine. I raised it. Somalis in the UK. The family of the couple. Various donors.

YOUNGER MAN. Where is it?

MAN. I have it.

YOUNGER MAN. You don't trust me. You want my help. I'm your nephew. But you don't trust me.

MAN. I'll take off the vest.

YOUNGER MAN. You promised your wife you'd keep it on.
Do you always break your promises so willingly?

MAN. I try not to make a habit of it.

I've always kept my promise to your father.

To send what I could, I've always done that.

YOUNGER MAN. We're very grateful.

MAN. I don't want your gratitude.

YOUNGER MAN. What do you want then?

MAN. I'd love you to help me. Help put me in touch with the
pirates holding the British couple.

YOUNGER MAN. Aren't they demanding five million pounds?

MAN. I've got nothing like that much, all I want is to talk to
them.

YOUNGER MAN. How much do you have?

MAN. It's not my money. But we've managed to raise half a
million.

YOUNGER MAN. Could you blame me if I was a pirate?

Pause.

Do you know these people?

The couple.

MAN. No.

YOUNGER MAN. That's probably like asking me if I know the
pirates isn't it? Why should you? You don't know everyone
in Britain do you.

MAN. No.

YOUNGER MAN. But you've come here to save them.

Pause.

MAN. It's better for everyone if they survive. For the couple of course, for the pirates, and for Somalia.

YOUNGER MAN. And for you, presumably.

MAN. For everyone.

YOUNGER MAN. Are you being paid to negotiate?

MAN. No.

YOUNGER MAN. You leave your job, your family, you come to this place and you're not being compensated in any way?

MAN. I wanted to come.

YOUNGER MAN. You didn't want to before.

Pause.

He told me not to tell you. As he was dying, it took a day or two, he told me not to tell you, because he'll want to come, he said, and he shouldn't waste his money.

I did tell you. But you didn't come.

MAN. I didn't have the money.

Pause.

It's hard here, but it's hard there too.

YOUNGER MAN. You wear that when you drive your Mercedes do you?

Pause.

MAN. Things have changed since I left.

YOUNGER MAN. Not really.

MAN. If you can just put me in touch with someone who might know something.

Pause.

I can pay.

YOUNGER MAN. We're family.

MAN. I can pay expenses, bribes, whatever you need.

YOUNGER MAN. You want me to be your guide in this strange and dangerous land.

MAN. I haven't forgotten everything.

YOUNGER MAN. Are you working for the British Government?

MAN. The Government?

YOUNGER MAN. They'll think you are.

MAN. I drive a minicab.

YOUNGER MAN. They'll think you are. If you say things like I can pay expenses, whatever you want, it sounds like you're working for the state.

MAN. I'm not.

YOUNGER MAN. How did you get the money to come here?

MAN. I borrowed it.

YOUNGER MAN. Or the Government paid.

MAN. I'm nothing to do with the Government.

YOUNGER MAN. Have you been to Number 10?

MAN. I've driven past.

YOUNGER MAN. Why could you borrow the money this time but you couldn't before?

MAN. They won't ask me that.

YOUNGER MAN. I'm asking.

Pause.

MAN. The situation's different now.

Pause.

I'm sorry I didn't come.

YOUNGER MAN. You're sorry now you need my help.

Pause.

You must earn a lot if you work for the Government.

MAN. I don't work for the Government. If you only knew how far from reality that is.

YOUNGER MAN. Do you want to work for the Government? Is this like an audition?

MAN. An audition? No.

YOUNGER MAN. Then what?

MAN. Shall I tell you?

I'll tell you what this is. My son, Cabaas

YOUNGER MAN. He's my cousin, I know his name.

MAN. Of course. Cabaas

YOUNGER MAN. How are they? Zahi and Cabaas? Alive and well?

MAN. Yes they're

They're well thank you.

YOUNGER MAN. But this is about Cabaas?

MAN. At school, he's

It's not just about Cabaas, it's the whole community, it's important for the whole community.

YOUNGER MAN. Which community?

MAN. To show our gratitude.

To do something to show the country we're

YOUNGER MAN. Like a test.

MAN. No. Not a test.

YOUNGER MAN. Like a present?

MAN. A what?

YOUNGER MAN. A gift to the British people. To save two of their own.

MAN. My own.

YOUNGER MAN. Do they know how you treat your own?

MAN. I've treated you fairly.

Pause.

What do you need?

YOUNGER MAN. In life or

MAN. Tell me what you need. I can help you get out of here.

YOUNGER MAN. Then why haven't you before?

Pause.

MAN. I'll be in a better position to help if

YOUNGER MAN. Oh and that's why you've come is it? To help me.

MAN. If you help me track these people down, as I've been saying, we'll all be in a stronger position.

YOUNGER MAN. My whole family?

MAN. Yes.

YOUNGER MAN. Maybe we don't want to leave.

MAN. Don't you?

YOUNGER MAN. What would you do then?

MAN. I think you'd leave if you could.

YOUNGER MAN. My father didn't leave.

MAN. And where is he now?

Pause.

Help me. Please.

Scene Five

YOUNGER MAN. I'd rather speak in English.

MAN. Not on my account.

YOUNGER MAN. No. I need the practice. And as a guy who's lived there, you'll know all the slang. I like slang.

MAN. My sons would probably be better for that kind of thing.

YOUNGER MAN. Are they here?

MAN. No.

YOUNGER MAN. Then you'll do.

Pause.

I've been trying to speak to the couple / but they're

MAN. How are they?

YOUNGER MAN. Okay. Why would they not be?

MAN. You're holding them hostage.

YOUNGER MAN. I'm not a thug.

What's another word for that?

MAN. Are they coping?

YOUNGER MAN. What's another word for that? I want to expand my vocabulary.

MAN. Why?

YOUNGER MAN. To get better of course. How else would you say it, thug?

MAN. I don't know.

YOUNGER MAN. You've come here for my help haven't you? You can give me a few words. What do the newspapers in Britain call us?

MAN. I don't know.

YOUNGER MAN. You won't offend me.

MAN. Pirates.

YOUNGER MAN. Is that all?

MAN. You're not in the news for long.

The Government won't give you the money.

YOUNGER MAN. There was an Australian man on a cargo
ship we captured and he called us crooks. I like that word.
We let him go. After they gave us two million dollars, but
also because he gave me a new word. Crook.

MAN. Your English is better than mine.

YOUNGER MAN. Thank you. Do they use this word in Britain
or is it just in Australia?

MAN. No, we use it too.

YOUNGER MAN. We?

MAN. I didn't realise this was going to be an English lesson.

YOUNGER MAN. You've travelled all the way here, you
might as well share what you have.

Pause.

MAN. Are you planning on coming to the UK?

YOUNGER MAN. Would they want me? A crook.

MAN. Is that what you want the money for? To get out of here.

YOUNGER MAN. Do I ask you why you have a job?

MAN. What you do isn't a job.

YOUNGER MAN. Oh, what is the right word for it?

Business?

You have come here to do business with me.

MAN. I've come here to negotiate with you.

YOUNGER MAN. Are they different?

MAN. I'm not an expert.

YOUNGER MAN. In language or in business?

MAN. Neither of them.

YOUNGER MAN. So why did they send you?

MAN. No one sent me here.

YOUNGER MAN. Then why did you come?

MAN. To help.

YOUNGER MAN. You can help by giving me the money we've asked for.

MAN. I can't do that.

YOUNGER MAN. Then you can't help.

MAN. I can give you some money.

YOUNGER MAN. How much?

MAN. A quarter of a million.

YOUNGER MAN. What is another word for idiot?

MAN. Stupid.

YOUNGER MAN. I know that word. Another word.

MAN. Fool.

YOUNGER MAN. I know that word. Another word.

MAN. I don't know.

YOUNGER MAN. Do you think I'm a moron?

MAN. No.

YOUNGER MAN. My Australian friend taught me moron.

MAN. He's not a friend if you capture him and hold him hostage.

YOUNGER MAN. I let him live. That was friendly wasn't it?

Pause.

MAN. I don't think you're a moron.

YOUNGER MAN. Good. Then maybe we can be friends.

MAN. No one sent me here. I went to the Somali community in the UK and I asked them to donate as much as they could. Which they did. I paid for a ticket and here I am. To negotiate.

YOUNGER MAN. There's nothing to negotiate if you only have two hundred and fifty thousand pounds.

MAN. It's better than nothing.

YOUNGER MAN. We want five million. A quarter of a million is an insult.

MAN. We don't have that much.

Pause.

YOUNGER MAN. What is your job?

MAN. I drive a cab.

YOUNGER MAN. You went all the way to London to drive a car?

What car do you drive?

MAN. A Ford Mondeo.

YOUNGER MAN. You went all the way to London to drive a Ford Mondeo?

No surprise you have come back.

MAN. It's a good job.

YOUNGER MAN. Maybe if you have a good car.

MAN. It's a good job.

YOUNGER MAN. Who do you drive?

MAN. People.

YOUNGER MAN. Government officials?

MAN. Businessmen. People like that.

YOUNGER MAN. People like me.

MAN. No.

YOUNGER MAN. If I came to London would you drive me around?

MAN. If you came to London and tried to do what you do here you'd never get away with it. It's a different kind of place.

YOUNGER MAN. London has no crooks?

MAN. If you came to London and demanded five million pounds for kidnapping someone they'd laugh at you.

YOUNGER MAN. Of course. I'd demand at least ten million if I was in London.

MAN. They'd track you down and put you away.

YOUNGER MAN. But I'm not in London.

And neither are you.

Pause.

MAN. I can think of lots of things I'd do with a quarter of a million pounds.

YOUNGER MAN. What?

MAN. Buy a house.

YOUNGER MAN. That's one thing.

MAN. A big thing.

YOUNGER MAN. Nearly fifty of us need to be paid. And we all have families who expect something.

MAN. The longer the negotiations go on the more everyone will expect.

YOUNGER MAN. I'm telling you if a quarter of a million is all you have then go right now.

Pause.

So you have more.

MAN. I can go a little higher, but not much.

YOUNGER MAN. How much is a little?

MAN. A hundred thousand.

YOUNGER MAN. Very little.

MAN. It's a lot here.

YOUNGER MAN. For people like us?

MAN. It goes further here than in other places.

YOUNGER MAN. How long have you been back?

MAN. Long enough to know the price of things.

YOUNGER MAN. And how long have you been away?

Pause.

How long have you been away?

MAN. I send money to my family, I know how much things
cost.

YOUNGER MAN. I give money to my family too. I can't do
that with four hundred thousand.

MAN. I said three hundred and fifty.

YOUNGER MAN. I can do even less with that.

Pause.

These people have a yacht. Their family can pay.

MAN. Their family have contributed but they're not
millionaires.

YOUNGER MAN. Would they give their money to you?

MAN. It's not for me, it's for you.

YOUNGER MAN. But would they trust you with it?

You look like me.

MAN. No I don't.

YOUNGER MAN. You're fatter. But to them, you look like me.

MAN. I'm not like you.

YOUNGER MAN. You look like me.

MAN. I went to them personally and I told them I wanted to bring their parents back.

YOUNGER MAN. What was their house like?

MAN. Normal.

YOUNGER MAN. Do they own it?

MAN. I didn't ask.

YOUNGER MAN. Why not?

MAN. Because it's rude.

YOUNGER MAN. You are coming here, to negotiate with pirates, with crooks, to save their parents. I think you can ask.

MAN. They were very upset. They gave what they have.

Pause.

YOUNGER MAN. You work for the Government?

MAN. No.

YOUNGER MAN. You drive a Ford Mondeo?

MAN. Yes.

YOUNGER MAN. I wouldn't give you my money.

MAN. Well they did. Which is what I'm offering you now.

YOUNGER MAN. How much do you have?

MAN. I've told you.

YOUNGER MAN. No. At first you had two hundred and fifty. After a few minutes you had three hundred and fifty. How much will you have in an hour?

MAN. If I worked for the Government I'd be better at this wouldn't I?

YOUNGER MAN. You could be pretending to be an idiot.

Pause.

MAN. These people were just on holiday. They weren't fishing in your waters. They weren't dumping toxic waste in your waters. They aren't a threat to you.

YOUNGER MAN. No.

MAN. So how can you justify holding them hostage?

YOUNGER MAN. They're British.

MAN. So am I.

YOUNGER MAN. Perhaps I should hold you hostage as well.

Pause.

Relax. I wouldn't do that.

If this is all I get for them, what would I get for you?

Silence.

Don't be upset. It's just business.

You're thinking, why did I come here?

So am I. If you only came with three hundred and fifty thousand.

MAN. I'm your only chance to make some money out of this.

YOUNGER MAN. I think so too.

That's why I'm not interested in peanuts.

The Australian taught me that. I like it.

MAN. Three hundred and fifty thousand pounds isn't peanuts.

YOUNGER MAN. It means a small amount, doesn't it?

MAN. That's not a small amount.

YOUNGER MAN. Divided by fifty it is. I want walnuts.

MAN. You can't say that.

YOUNGER MAN. You know what I mean don't you?

Pause.

What slang would your sons teach me?

MAN. I don't know.

YOUNGER MAN. Words they don't use with you.

MAN. I don't know.

YOUNGER MAN. Words they use with their friends.

Do they have many friends?

Pause.

MAN. Five million is unreasonable.

YOUNGER MAN. Is it? For two lives?

MAN. You must expect to compromise.

YOUNGER MAN. I don't like that word.

MAN. You say you're not a thug.

What do you imagine people think of you?

YOUNGER MAN. People don't think of me.

Do you imagine they think of you?

If you save this pair they might.

They might call you a hero.

They might invite you to Buckingham Palace for afternoon tea.

I think you need to offer more than three hundred and fifty for that.

MAN. It's all I have.

YOUNGER MAN. I don't believe you.

How many times have you driven past Buckingham Palace in your Ford Mondeo? I bet you'd like to go in.

MAN. Do you imagine you're helping Somalia?

YOUNGER MAN. I don't spend much time imagining.

MAN. How will we ever get anywhere if people like you continue to do whatever you want?

YOUNGER MAN. I don't want to get anywhere. I am somewhere. I'm here.

MAN. And what kind of life can you have here?

YOUNGER MAN. Do you imagine you're helping Somalia by leaving?

You're helping yourself. Not Somalia. Just like you're helping yourself by coming back.

MAN. I could help you too, but you won't let me.

YOUNGER MAN. Three hundred and / fifty isn't

MAN. What's the least you'll accept?

YOUNGER MAN. Do you think I'm a moron?

MAN. Do you think I am?

YOUNGER MAN. Yes.

MAN. Well I'm not. I will walk away and you will have nothing. Don't think I won't walk away. You should be careful.

YOUNGER MAN. You're threatening a pirate?

I could kill you as well as the couple.

MAN. Then you would definitely be a thug.

YOUNGER MAN. A businessman.

If I kill you and them, next time, I will definitely get the money I ask for.

MAN. Or prison.

You accepted two million before. With the cargo ship. This is a small sailing boat. You only have two hostages. You can't expect to get five million.

YOUNGER MAN. Inflation.

MAN. That was less than a year ago.

Pause.

Is there someone else I can speak to?

YOUNGER MAN. Why? Don't you like me?

MAN. You think I'm a moron. You won't negotiate with me.
Fine. Is there someone who will?

YOUNGER MAN. You take it personally?

MAN. I'm not an idiot. Do you think it's easy to leave? Do you
think it's easy, it isn't easy, and that's why you haven't done it.

YOUNGER MAN. Do you want a medal?

MAN. I don't want anything from you.

YOUNGER MAN. That's not true.

Pause.

MAN. I don't.

I don't want anything from you.

YOUNGER MAN. I can't accept less than three million.

Pause.

Do not smile.

MAN. At first you wanted five million. After ten minutes you'll
take three. How much will you accept in an hour?

Pause.

YOUNGER MAN. You don't want to go back without the
couple. What would you say to the people who gave you
money? What would you say to your sons?

MAN. I tried. That's more than anyone else.

YOUNGER MAN. But you don't want to say that.

Do you get invited to Buckingham Palace for trying?

MAN. I don't know what you have to do.

YOUNGER MAN. Do you have three million?

MAN. No.

YOUNGER MAN. Then why are you smiling?

Pause.

Do you negotiate your cab fares?

MAN. No.

YOUNGER MAN. Why not?

MAN. There are fixed prices.

YOUNGER MAN. So you thought you'd practise with a pirate instead?

MAN. This isn't practice, I don't want a career in this. I don't want to do this again. I'm only doing it to help the Clarkes get home.

YOUNGER MAN. If that's all you want why didn't you pay a professional?

MAN. I don't need a professional qualification to come here and speak to my people.

YOUNGER MAN. You said you are British.

MAN. And you said I look the same as you.

Can we speak in Somali?

YOUNGER MAN. Why?

MAN. It's our language.

YOUNGER MAN. I've told you, I want to learn English slang. But you don't know much.

MAN. I want to speak our language.

YOUNGER MAN. I speak it all the time.

The couple don't know much either.

Too old I suppose.

Pause.

MAN. Can I see them?

YOUNGER MAN. You think they're dead?

MAN. I'd like to see them. So they know they're not alone.

YOUNGER MAN. There are always guards with them. They know they're not alone.

MAN. I mean, so they know we're trying to help them.

YOUNGER MAN. You think they want to see your face?

Your face is like my face.

How will they know you're not one of us?

MAN. Their children wanted me to pass on a message.

YOUNGER MAN. Why didn't their children come here themselves?

MAN. Because it's

Because I came.

YOUNGER MAN. They let you come because it doesn't matter if we kill you.

MAN. They trusted me to come for them.

YOUNGER MAN. They let you come because they're scared.

MAN. Yes they're scared.

Their parents are being held by pirates. Of course they're scared.

Their parents are in some crazy African country that is only ever in the news for pirates or war or death.

They are terrified.

I didn't need to ask them if they own their house. I know they've given me everything they have.

YOUNGER MAN. What is the message?

MAN. It's for their parents.

YOUNGER MAN. What is the message?

MAN. I'm sure you can guess what it is.

YOUNGER MAN. Tell me.

MAN. What do you think it might be?

YOUNGER MAN. Tell me.

MAN. Let me tell them.

YOUNGER MAN. You ask for a lot and don't give me anything.

MAN. I've offered three hundred and fifty thousand pounds.
    Cash. Not a pie in the sky, but real cash.

YOUNGER MAN. Pie in the sky?

MAN. Three million is a pie in the sky.

YOUNGER MAN. Is that slang?

MAN. It means it's a dream. Not going to happen. And you
    know it.

YOUNGER MAN. I like it. Pie in the sky.

Pause.

Were they crying? Their children.

MAN. No.

YOUNGER MAN. Their grandchildren?

MAN. I didn't meet them.

YOUNGER MAN. Why not?

MAN. They're very young. They don't understand what's
    happening.

YOUNGER MAN. They kept them from you.

MAN. Why would they do that?

YOUNGER MAN. You should be an honoured guest. They should line up to kiss your feet. But you're just a messenger.

MAN. They're terrified. I don't expect them to wait on me.

YOUNGER MAN. But when you get back?

Pause.

I know what it's like when people take advantage of you.

MAN. They're not taking advantage of me. I offered to come here.

YOUNGER MAN. And they let you.

I know what it's like.

But I'm standing up for myself now.

MAN. Is that what this is?

The Clarkes weren't taking advantage of you.

YOUNGER MAN. But they're taking advantage of you.

Don't let them.

Don't let them take advantage of either of us. I can't accept three hundred and fifty.

Let's work together.

It's what they expect.

You could buy a house. I could build a house.

Brother.

They sent you out here to die.

MAN. No.

YOUNGER MAN. You told me. All they know of Somalia is pirates and death. So what do you think will happen to you?

They expect you to die. Or to cheat them. Which would you prefer?

If we are organised, this could be a successful business.

MAN. Why did they give me their money?

YOUNGER MAN. Some money. An amount they can lose. *gamble.

MAN. It's more than that.

YOUNGER MAN. How much?

Pause.

They have a yacht.

MAN. That's all they have.

They believe you would kill them. Why would they gamble with their parents' lives?

YOUNGER MAN. You don't know them.

Maybe they don't like their parents.

MAN. They're close.

YOUNGER MAN. Then why are they sailing the seas?

MAN. For adventure.

YOUNGER MAN. Maybe to get away from their family.

Is that why you left?

MAN. No.

YOUNGER MAN. You did leave your family behind?

MAN. But I didn't forget them.

YOUNGER MAN. You didn't come back here to help strangers.

I don't think so.

We can make a lot of money brother.

I think you have more than you say. Of course you want to keep some for yourself. You are not an idiot. But if we work together, you can get even more than you imagined.

You like imagining.

Pause.

lion. That's all.

p any for myself.

: .

ısand pounds is everything.

YOUNGER MAN. I don't believe you.

MAN. That's a shame.

YOUNGER MAN. What do you say brother?

Scene Six

MAN. They've treated you well enough?

Pause.

They're not thugs.

I know you might not think that at the moment, but they could've done a lot worse.

They just want money. Now we've given them money and we can go.

We've still got to get across the border, and it's dangerous until then but

It should be over soon.

You don't believe it, I'm sure, and that's understandable.

I asked to see you before but they wouldn't let me. I wanted you to know you weren't alone.

WOMAN. Who are you?

MAN. I've been negotiating for your release.

WOMAN. Where are you from?

Pause.

YOUNGER MAN. Where are you from?

MAN. I live in London.

WOMAN. You're a Somali?

MAN. I've lived in the UK for twenty years.

I went to see your children. They paid some of the ransom.

WOMAN. You saw our children?

MAN. I went to your daughter's house.

YOUNGER MAN. They can't afford to pay a ransom like that.

MAN. They contributed some.

WOMAN. She's got a baby on the way.

YOUNGER MAN. They can't afford that kind of money.

MAN. I didn't beat it out of them.

Pause.

Their friends and family, your friends and family, all contributed. They were inundated they said.

Pause.

And the Somali community wanted to help. People you've never met.

We're not all crooks.

YOUNGER MAN. You understand why we're finding this hard to

MAN. Of course I can understand. It's a shock.

YOUNGER MAN. We've never seen you before and you come to us and

WOMAN. They separated us, for a month. I couldn't survive that again.

MAN. I'm not here to separate you.

YOUNGER MAN. You understand we've never met you.

MAN. I understand that, yes.

YOUNGER MAN. You understand it's difficult for us to know who to trust at this stage.

MAN. Your children wanted me to pass on a message.

WOMAN. What is it?

YOUNGER MAN. What did they say?

WOMAN. No, wait, I need to

YOUNGER MAN. Tell us.

MAN. They'll be able to tell you themselves soon but

YOUNGER MAN. What is it?

Pause.

MAN. They love you.

Pause.

WOMAN. Okay.

YOUNGER MAN. Was there anything more?

MAN. More?

YOUNGER MAN. You understand that, obviously, you could just tell us that

WOMAN. It doesn't take a genius to come up with

YOUNGER MAN. You could just say that because obviously that's what people say.

MAN. There was nothing else to say.

WOMAN. But if that's supposed to convince us that you met with our children then

MAN. It's not supposed to convince you of anything. It's a message.

YOUNGER MAN. Did they say anything more personal?

MAN. They love you. That was the message.

YOUNGER MAN. Did they give you something perhaps?

MAN. Yes. Money. To free you.

Pause.

YOUNGER MAN. Please don't think we're

WOMAN. When are we leaving?

MAN. Any minute, they're just organising the car.

WOMAN. How are we supposed to know this isn't a trap?

MAN. I don't know.

I can describe your daughter's house, would that help?

WOMAN. Even if you've been to her house, what does that prove?

MAN. I could make up a longer message? Was it just the length you didn't like?

WOMAN. Anyone could've

YOUNGER MAN. Darling, we need to

WOMAN. Do you work for the Government?

MAN. No.

WOMAN. Then who are you? What do you do?

MAN. I'm a cab driver.

WOMAN. A cab driver, I don't

YOUNGER MAN. Can you understand why

MAN. Yes I understand.

WOMAN. What are you doing here?

MAN. I came here to help you.

Pause.

YOUNGER MAN. Please don't think we're not

MAN. Why would I think that?

YOUNGER MAN. You understand

MAN. Of course I understand, I'm not an idiot.

But I came here to help you. Can you understand that?

I've been negotiating for more than a month.

I'm not from the Government because it refuses to negotiate with pirates. And I'm not an undercover agent.

Please don't look at me like that.

WOMAN. I'm not.

MAN. Like you're trying to remember if you've seen me before.

If I'm one of them.

I'm not.

YOUNGER MAN. She's not looking at you like / that.

MAN. I'm not one of them.

All I've tried to do is help.

We're going home.

YOUNGER MAN. Now?

MAN. Now.

WOMAN. How much did you

MAN. One point two million.

WOMAN. One point two

They were asking for five.

MAN. We negotiated.

YOUNGER MAN. Where did you get it?

WOMAN. Who would

MAN. I told you. Your family. The Somalis in the UK. Some of us are successful business people, they wanted to contribute.

WOMAN. But they don't even know us.

MAN. I don't know you.

WOMAN. Exactly.

You just heard about us on the news and thought, I'll go and help?

MAN. It was my sons.

I wanted to give them something to be proud of.

YOUNGER MAN. Please don't be offended that we're

You understand we're

Sorry, I know you understand, I didn't mean it like

It's just it's been us, you see, and them. And now you're here and

MAN. And I look like them.

YOUNGER MAN. No, that's not it. But we've been so

WOMAN. I won't survive if they separate us again.

MAN. They don't need you any more, they've got their money.

WOMAN. I thought they'd kill us.

MAN. They aren't thugs.

YOUNGER MAN. It's been us, together, for so long and all of a sudden it's over, that's it, and

MAN. Not all of a sudden.

YOUNGER MAN. No, but for us, we've been, we had no idea what was happening so now you come and tell us we're free but it's hard to believe, even if you were the Prime Minister it'd, it'd still be hard to take in.

MAN. You'd believe the Prime Minister.

YOUNGER MAN. I believe you.

MAN. Do you?

WOMAN. Will they tell us? Is someone going to come and tell us or is that it?

MAN. I'm telling you.

WOMAN. Yes, but the men we've seen day in day out.

MAN. What do you want, a farewell party?

WOMAN. For all we know

YOUNGER MAN. Darling.

WOMAN. No, but for all we know he's a pirate from another gang, you're a rival pirate and you've come to take us to your camp and then it starts all over again.

YOUNGER MAN. This situation makes you, you can understand how it makes you

MAN. What would convince you?

   The car's about to come and we'll drive to the border, will that convince you?

YOUNGER MAN. We probably won't believe it until we're back on home soil.

WOMAN. If we get there.

MAN. I want to get back as much as you.

YOUNGER MAN. Of course you do, to see your sons.

WOMAN. Where do you live?

MAN. East London.

WOMAN. Where?

MAN. Do you want my address?

YOUNGER MAN. Darling

WOMAN. They told us we were free before, then they changed their minds, they wanted more money, why should this time be any different?

MAN. You have my word.

WOMAN. Oh, well then.

MAN. Please don't say it like that.

YOUNGER MAN. We're exhausted, we're

WOMAN. I want to see green trees.

MAN. You will.

WOMAN. I hate this fucking country.

Do you hear me? I hate it.

MAN. You'll be back in yours soon.

YOUNGER MAN. I'm sorry she

WOMAN. Don't apologise for me.

YOUNGER MAN. He doesn't have to be here.

Your sons will be proud of you, I'm sure.

The whole country.

There aren't words

MAN. There are.

YOUNGER MAN. Of course thank you but that hardly seems

MAN. I don't want thank-yous.

YOUNGER MAN. You've saved our lives.

MAN. The money saved your lives. Lots of people gave the money.

YOUNGER MAN. But you came here when you didn't have to, you came here and you don't even know us.

WOMAN. We're not home yet.

YOUNGER MAN. But we're going home aren't we?

MAN. Yes.

YOUNGER MAN. Because this man, this Good Samaritan, decided not to turn his back. He's like an angel, we're not religious, but

There aren't words.

Are you real?

MAN. Yes.

YOUNGER MAN. Is this real?

MAN. Yes.

YOUNGER MAN. Is the car real?

MAN. It's a Toyota Surf.

YOUNGER MAN. We're going home.

MAN (*to* WOMAN). Do you believe it?

WOMAN. When I'm home maybe.

MAN. But you'll get in the car?

YOUNGER MAN. Of course we'll get in the car.

MAN. You'll get in the car?

YOUNGER MAN. Of course.

MAN. I'm not going to force you Mrs Clarke.

I came here to bring you home, but I won't force you to come with me.

YOUNGER MAN. A rival pirate wouldn't be asking.

MAN. I'm asking, I'm not forcing. The car will come and we'll have to leave. I came here to bring you back.

YOUNGER MAN. Of course we'll get in the car with you, won't we?

Scene Seven

WOMAN. We've said we're going.

MAN. I know what we said.

WOMAN. They've organised the whole thing for you.

MAN. It's for them.

WOMAN. They want to meet your family. The boys.

MAN. Zahi's got exams.

WOMAN. He can take an afternoon off.

MAN. Does he want to?

WOMAN. Why wouldn't he?

MAN. Have you even asked the boys if they want to go?

WOMAN. I thought the whole point was for them to

MAN. Have you asked them?

WOMAN. They want to meet the people their father saved.

MAN. Why? They're nothing special.

WOMAN. Don't say that.

MAN. They aren't.

WOMAN. I like her. We've only spoken on the phone but I like her.

MAN. They're ordinary.

WOMAN. Well you thought they were special enough to risk your life to save them.

MAN. I didn't risk my life.

WOMAN. Anything could've happened to you.

MAN. I went and spoke to my nephew, my family, friends of his. Is that risking my life?

WOMAN. Don't downplay what you did.

MAN. I went and spoke to some people. That's what I did.

WOMAN. Those people happened to be pirates.

MAN. They're not bloodthirsty cannibals Sabo. They just want money. Like the rest of us.

WOMAN. They just want to show their appreciation. Can't you let them do that?

MAN. Haven't I done enough for them already?

WOMAN. Exactly, and that's why they want to thank you.

MAN. So I have to go to their house, my family and I have to go to their house and what?

WOMAN. Eat some lunch. Chat. Is it really so painful?

MAN. We've got nothing in common.

WOMAN. You've never been shy.

MAN. I'm not shy.

WOMAN. You've never been antisocial.

MAN. I just don't particularly want to be their best friends.

WOMAN. You don't have to be.

MAN. They just happened to be in the wrong place at the wrong time, that doesn't make them interesting.

WOMAN. It's lunch. That's all.

MAN. That's not all though, is it. Now their daughter wants to name her son after me.

WOMAN. It's supposed to be an honour.

MAN. My name hardly fits that baby.

WOMAN. She obviously thinks it does.

MAN. But it's not just going to be lunch is it? If their grandson has my name. That's more than lunch.

WOMAN. Is that so terrible?

Pause.

I want to go.

MAN. Go then.

WOMAN. With you.

MAN. Go. They'll fall all over you I'm sure.

Pause.

WOMAN. You left me and you could've died. You left us to help them. So I'm not going to apologise for enjoying / some of the

MAN. Basking in the

WOMAN. What?

Basking?

MAN. In the reflected glory.

WOMAN. You think I'm, you think that's what I'm

MAN. You've been on the phone to her a lot.

WOMAN. To arrange today.

This false modesty is boring Dalmar.

MAN. False modesty?

WOMAN. Yes. It's boring. You know you'll come to their lunch and you know you'll enjoy it so I don't know why you have to make me beg you to go.

MAN. You're not begging me to go.

WOMAN. Not yet.

MAN. It's just lunch.

WOMAN. Exactly.

Pause.

The boys are proud of you.

MAN. That's all I wanted.

I don't want lunch.

WOMAN. You're my husband. We support each other, don't we? I didn't want you to go but you did, and I looked after the boys while you were off, and I really don't appreciate you suggesting that now you're back I'm trying to steal the

If you don't go, I'm not going.

It hasn't been over the top, considering what you did, they just want to show their gratitude. This is a positive story, for once, and people want to embrace that a bit, so I don't know why you, why you won't.

MAN. I have. I've smiled for the camera, I've done interviews.

Pause.

WOMAN. You haven't gone back to work yet.

If you really wanted everything to go back to normal, for us to forget all about it, you would've gone back to work.

MAN. I want to do this again.

WOMAN. What?

MAN. Negotiate.

WOMAN. You want to go back there?

MAN. There? It's our home.

WOMAN. This is our home.

MAN. I can do more than drive a car.

WOMAN. You like your job.

MAN. I can do more.

WOMAN. Well now's the moment to try. A few more doors might be open to you right now.

MAN. And in a year or two?

WOMAN. Now's the time to be thinking about what you want to do.

MAN. Should I ask the Clarkes to write my reference?

WOMAN. You can ask them at lunch.

MAN. This man saved us from pirates. We recommend you
    employ him.

WOMAN. At least you'd stand out from the crowd.

    Pause.

MAN. There are opportunities at home not open to me here.

WOMAN. Why? Because people get kidnapped by pirates.

    We can't go back.

MAN. We always said

WOMAN. I know what we said, but realistically Dalmar

MAN. I can help people there.

WOMAN. You can help people here.

MAN. Driving a cab for peanuts?

WOMAN. We get by.

    You don't have to go back to that.

MAN. I'm not going back to it.

    Pause.

WOMAN. I saw your boss on the news the other day, singing
    your praises, such a hard worker, natural rapport with the
    customers. You should let him know if you're not going back.

MAN. Natural rapport?

WOMAN. You know you do, you can get on with anyone.

    Even pirates.

MAN. The pirates didn't hand over the Clarkes because they
    liked me. What do you imagine, I waltz in, tell a few jokes
    and they let them go? It's just about the money. That's all.

WOMAN. Why do you keep downplaying what you've done?

MAN. Why do you keep going on about it?

WOMAN. Someone's got to.

MAN. Why?

I'm going back out there. I don't want to be some kind of
celebrity, it'll make it harder, they'll think I have important
friends, they'll demand more.

WOMAN. You're going back?

Pause.

When?

MAN. Next week.

WOMAN. You've only just got home.

Who have they kidnapped now?

MAN. There are always hostages.

WOMAN. Are they British?

MAN. Does that matter?

WOMAN. I thought that was

I didn't realise this was going to become your job.

MAN. I think I can help and I want to so

WOMAN. Are you getting paid?

MAN. We'll be fine, you don't need to worry.

WOMAN. How will we be fine?

People looked after us while you were away, they were very
generous, but we can't expect them to do that for good.

MAN. Have I ever expected anything of them?

Have you ever known me to do that?

WOMAN. No.

MAN. I've taken whatever jobs I had to take to support us and I
haven't complained once, so why, all of a sudden, would
you, my wife of all people, think that I'm going to leave you
to rely on handouts? Why would you think that?

Pause.

You should go to lunch.

It might be the last good meal you get in a while.

Pause.

WOMAN. The community rallied round, that's all I meant.

MAN. I know they did and I'm grateful.

WOMAN. Stuck together.

MAN. Yes.

WOMAN. Our people.

MAN. And I got them what they wanted didn't I? The Clarkes made it back safe and sound.

WOMAN. I thought that's what you wanted.

MAN. It was.

WOMAN. All you wanted.

But now you're back and you're telling me we'll be fine, don't worry, when you always worry, and now you're going back there and

MAN. You'll be late for lunch.

WOMAN. I'm not hungry.

MAN. Then don't go, I don't care.

WOMAN. Do you care what the boys think?

MAN. I can't imagine they'll be upset at missing lunch with a family they don't know.

WOMAN. What kind of example is it?

MAN. To miss lunch?

Pause.

You go.

WOMAN. And have to listen to how grateful they are and what a great man you are and

MAN. They're back with their family aren't they? They're free aren't they? They can hold their new grandson can't they?

WOMAN. Their new grandson Dalmar.

Pause.

You didn't go out there to make money.

MAN. So I should ignore an opportunity that comes my way?

Pause.

WOMAN. How much?

MAN. It's for the boys.

WOMAN. Please don't try to

And you accuse me of basking in

And when it comes out, which it will?

MAN. No one will be surprised. It's what they all expect anyway.

WOMAN. It'll be even worse than before.

Any good will be forgotten, and it'll be worse.

You have to go to the lunch. It'll look strange

MAN. Say I'm sick.

WOMAN. It'll look strange.

MAN. And if I go I'll be accused of basking in / the glory

WOMAN. They invited us, no one's going to accuse you of

MAN. Of playing the hero. They will. How dare he, he was only sorting out a mess any self-respecting, he was only going back to the country he was born, does that make him a hero? Heroes go to places unknown, dangerous places, but he just went back to his village, to his people, it's an abuse of the word, it cheapens the word for all the true

And if I don't go, it looks strange you say, even my wife thinks it'll look strange, but people change plans all the time.

Maybe I'm sick, why wouldn't they believe me? I might've picked up an obscure parasitic disease, doctors baffled, riddled with the things, perhaps it was the water, or maybe there was a girl, away from home, not home but, away from it all, might've been a girl, or some, no, beast, no, too extreme, probably just a general lack of hygiene, simple, more likely, came on all of a sudden. You could say that and it could be true, in fact they'd probably love it, hero dying of, no not hero, man, Briton, Briton dying of deadly, tragic but satisfying end to the, but you're telling me that would be strange, fine.

So tell me what looks natural, Sabo, what looks okay, what looks like I'm innocent, just a normal man, who happened to do something for other people without a

Tell me.

Scene Eight

YOUNGER MAN. Did you meet the guy?

MAN. You'll have to be more specific.

YOUNGER MAN. The one who looked like Cabaas.

MAN. I met a lot of people.

YOUNGER MAN. I'm sure you'd remember him, he's the spitting image of / your son.

MAN. Photos can be deceptive.

YOUNGER MAN. Did you meet him?

MAN. There was no formal introduction or

YOUNGER MAN. But you saw him?

Pause.

MAN. He didn't look that similar.

YOUNGER MAN. He must've. If you knew it was him.

MAN. You're too clever for your own good.

YOUNGER MAN. No such thing.

MAN. I hope it's reflected in your results.

YOUNGER MAN. Nice try Dad.

　　Did you speak to him? Cabaas's double.

MAN. He certainly wasn't his double.

YOUNGER MAN. Lookalike then.

MAN. I wasn't there to speak to the guards Zahi.

YOUNGER MAN. But this one looks exactly / like

MAN. He's nothing like Cabaas. Alright?

　　Pause.

YOUNGER MAN. What's he like then?

MAN. He's a guard, he has an AK47 and a job to do.

YOUNGER MAN. Did you speak to him?

MAN. Why are you so interested?

YOUNGER MAN. Cabaas was freaked out by it.

MAN. There's no reason to be, they don't look similar in
　　real life.

YOUNGER MAN. He looks like he could be my brother.

MAN. He's not your

YOUNGER MAN. He looks like he could be.

　　How old is he?

MAN. How should I know Zahi?

YOUNGER MAN. Guess.

MAN. Eighteen. I don't know. Not old.

YOUNGER MAN. What's his name?

MAN. I can't remember.

How do you think your exams went?

YOUNGER MAN. Dad.

MAN. What Zahi? I really don't see how we can have a conversation about a boy I know nothing about. I can't tell you when he was born, or what he likes, or how many brothers and sisters he has, I'm sorry.

How did the exams go?

YOUNGER MAN. Impossible to know.

MAN. You seem to know everything else.

Pause.

Mum says you worked hard.

YOUNGER MAN. I could come with you.

MAN. What?

YOUNGER MAN. I want to meet him.

MAN. Why on earth would you want to meet him?

YOUNGER MAN. Now my exams are done, I've got the summer, I could come with you.

MAN. It's not a holiday Zahi.

YOUNGER MAN. I could help you.

MAN. Your mother needs you here.

YOUNGER MAN. No she doesn't.

MAN. Cabaas needs / his brother.

YOUNGER MAN. If he can manage without you he can manage without me.

Pause.

I could help you. He's pretty much my age, we can talk and

MAN. They're pirates Zahi. What exactly do you think you'll talk about?

Pause.

You were going to get a job this summer.

YOUNGER MAN. Doing what? Handing out flyers, serving fries?

MAN. It's money.

YOUNGER MAN. Yeah but how much more experience could I get with you. You can't even compare them.

Imagine writing that in a personal statement. I negotiated with pirates last summer. Loads of transferable skills.

MAN. You could also be killed.

YOUNGER MAN. I could meet family I've never met.

MAN. It's not a holiday.

YOUNGER MAN. They helped you get in touch with the pirates didn't they? I could get to know them. I should, don't you think?

MAN. Your family's here. And your mother won't allow it.

YOUNGER MAN. Didn't stop you.

And that's good 'cause what you did was

When we went to that lunch, the woman gave me her scrawny white baby, Dalmar, to hold, and they were all like, doesn't he look like your dad? And I laughed 'cause I thought they were joking but they weren't. Babies don't look like anyone, but even if they did how could he look like you, why would he, but they're so, I don't know the word, but they feel so in debt they really think this baby looks like you.

I know I could help you Dad.

I can talk to these guys like they're Cabaas.

MAN. Why? Because they bear a resemblance

    Boys like that aren't the ones who make the decisions. They just hold the guns. You could talk to him all you like, it doesn't mean the hostages would be released.

    It's about money Zahi. That's all it is.

YOUNGER MAN. Not for you.

    You could make money here if that's all you wanted.

    Pause.

MAN. They don't want to be your friends and they won't even talk to you unless you've got something to give.

    And I suppose, why should they?

YOUNGER MAN. They must've trusted you though, they must've felt a connection, otherwise they wouldn't have dealt with you, they didn't deal with anyone else.

MAN. Because no one else was offering.

YOUNGER MAN. They still didn't have to negotiate with you.

MAN. They didn't have a lot of choice.

    Pause.

    I don't know how long I'll be there. There's no set format for this kind of thing. And you'll have to be back to start college.

YOUNGER MAN. If I get the grades.

MAN. Of course you'll get the grades.

YOUNGER MAN. If I want to go.

MAN. You've always wanted to go.

YOUNGER MAN. You didn't go to college and look what you're doing. You're doing something that matters.

    You've got people naming their children after you.

MAN. Not people. One couple.

YOUNGER MAN. Still.

MAN. Am I supposed to be grateful for that too now?

YOUNGER MAN. I don't think they expect you / to be

MAN. It's one couple, caught up in the emotion of it, if the baby was born in six months I doubt they would've been calling it

YOUNGER MAN. Well I think it's nice.

MAN. Nice?

YOUNGER MAN. Well I don't think they meant it to annoy you.

MAN. It hasn't annoyed me I just

YOUNGER MAN. You haven't even gone to see him.

MAN. I will.

YOUNGER MAN. You're leaving tomorrow.

MAN. When I'm back.

YOUNGER MAN. You don't even know when that'll be.

MAN. Which is why I need you here.

Please, Zahi. Get a job, it doesn't matter if it's boring, in a few years you'll be doing something you want to be doing and you can look back and think, look how far I've come.

Stay here and do that for me?

I don't want you getting caught up in anything.

YOUNGER MAN. What do you imagine I'm going to do, become a pirate?

MAN. No.

YOUNGER MAN. You think I'm a baby.

MAN. Not a baby, a boy.

YOUNGER MAN. Maybe I want a bit of adventure.

MAN. You think fraternising with pirates is an adventure?

YOUNGER MAN. What is it then?

MAN. You won't be fraternising with them at all.

   Ask the Clarkes how they enjoyed it.

YOUNGER MAN. They're safe now aren't they?

MAN. So you envy them?

YOUNGER MAN. Well they've got a story to tell the grandkids now, haven't they?

MAN. And do you envy the boy in the photo, is that what this obsession is?

YOUNGER MAN. Not envy but

MAN. Nothing. He has nothing and you envy him?

YOUNGER MAN. He gets paid doesn't he?

   Pause.

MAN. Why do you think I came here? For adventure? Is that how you imagine it was, I thought I'd just take to the seas one day, see where I ended up, like the Clarkes perhaps, why not, I was young, the world was my

   No.

   And I'm not going back there for adventure either.

   But if that's what you want then I'll send you off on your own Zahi, would you like that? You go instead of me because I don't really want to go back there, if I'm honest with you, I don't want to go.

YOUNGER MAN. You don't have to.

MAN. We'll go down to the park I used to take you to, and we'll get one of those rowing boats we sometimes hired and we'll take it to the coast and you see how far you get. Would you like that? You want a story for your personal statement? To show how strong and independent you are, well off you go. I'll shake your hand and call you a man if you make it back.

Come on. Let's get your things together.

You go instead of me. Is that what you want?

YOUNGER MAN. I want to go with you.

MAN. No, no, it doesn't work like that, you don't get to choose, that's not how it is. You can't take me and you can't take Cabaas, you're on your own.

Pause.

And if you make it some place, you didn't die, well done, but you're going to have to forget that park and the lake where we rowed the boat because if you don't it's going to be

The thing is Zahi when you get in the boat, you're

Survival is the number-one thing. And when you get some place that remains, and that's good of course, because you need something to aim for, but when that's all, there's no, you lose something of, it's not an adventure, there's no point me telling you any of this.

Go then.

A Nick Hern Book

The Initiate first published in Great Britain in 2014 as a paperback original by
Nick Hern Books Limited, The Glasshouse, 49a Goldhawk Road, London W12 8QP
in association with Paines Plough

Cover image: Phoebe Cheong
Cover design: Ned Hoste, 2H

Typeset by Nick Hern Books, London
Printed in Great Britain by CPI Group (UK) Ltd

A CIP catalogue record for this book is available from the British Library

ISBN 978 1 84842 433 3